Looking Beyond Your Problems!

Birister Sharma

Dedicated to my loving wife....

Pallabi Devi Sharma

I surrendered to you, O my
Lord......

"Om Namah Shivaya"

Table of Contents

One Word

Everything is temporary in this world.

Everything has its own beginning and ending. Everything has its own expiry period.

This is the law of this world.

Your life is also temporary in this world.

You'll have to leave this world when your final day arrives.

Every moment is important for you.

Every moment counts in your life. Therefore, do whatever you want to do in your life.

Don't postpone anything for tomorrow.

Do it right now, since tomorrow never comes.

You've to live now; you've to act now.

Make every moment of your life special and memorable.

Don't waste your valuable time on unwanted and unnecessary things.

Don't weep for unwanted things.

Make your life purposeful and meaningful.

Do something great for yourself.

Make your own identity.

Exemplify your greatness with your great deeds.

Make your own history before you leave this world.

1. Everything is Temporary

Nothing is permanent in this world. Everything is temporary in this world. This is the reality of this world. You have to accept this reality.

There is a duration of time for everything. Everything is valid for its duration of time. Nothing will remain permanent in this world. Time will decide everything.

Therefore, don't live in the delusion that everything is permanent in your life. Everything will change with time. Everybody will leave you one day.

If everything is temporary, it doesn't mean that you'll stop living your life right from today, but this is the reality of this world, and you have to accept this reality.

You have to make your own life meaningful and purposeful. You have to make your own life more valuable and rich. You have to make every moment of your life special and memorable.

Q. Can you guarantee anything permanent in your life?

No. You can't guarantee anything permanent in your life.

For instance, if your health is sound and healthy today, you can't guarantee that in the coming days, weeks, months, and years, your health will remain in the same state. You may get sick or you may become weak.

But, yes, if you're able to maintain your regular balanced diet, work out, and maintain a good lifestyle, then, no doubt, you'll remain sound and healthy.

Q. Can you wear one pair of clothes permanently for your whole lifetime?

No. You can't wear one pair of clothes permanently for your whole lifetime.

Your clothes are not permanent. Your clothes will wear out over time. You have to wear different pairs of clothes as time changes. Even, you may be unable to remember how many pairs of clothes you've worn to date.

Q. Are all the seasons permanent throughout the year?

No.

All the seasons change throughout the year, one after another. After every summer season, the winter season arrives; and after every autumn season, the spring season arrives. These are the cycles of the seasons.

Summer season ⇋ Winter season

Autumn season ⇋ Spring season

In a similar way, your life is not permanent. Your life is like the changing seasons. It is a continuous cycle of change.

You can't stop it. But you can move on in order to enjoy the flavors of every season of your life.

Your happiness is not permanent.

Your sorrow is not permanent.

These are the continuous cycles of change.

Therefore, try to enjoy your life.

Don't worry about anything.

Just do your work with heart and soul.

Keep your spirits high and have patience.

Nothing will remain permanent.

Happiness ⇋ Sorrow

Your success is not permanent.

Your failure is not permanent.

These are the continuous cycles of change.

Therefore, try to enjoy your life.

Don't worry about anything.

Just do your work with heart and soul.

Keep your spirits high and have patience.

Nothing will remain permanent.

Success ⇋ Failure

Your prosperity is not permanent.

Your adversity is not permanent.

These are the continuous cycles of change.

Therefore, try to enjoy your life.

Don't worry about anything.

Just do your work with heart and soul.

Keep your spirits high and have patience.

Nothing will remain permanent.

Prosperity ⇋ Adversity

There are four stages of a man:

First stage: An infant

Second stage: A young boy

Third stage: A young man

Fourth stage: An old man

An Infant → A Young Boy → A Young Man → An Old Man

You can't stop the stages of your life. You're bound to cross all four stages of your life (an infant, a young boy, a young man, and an old man). You can't stop the changing process of your life.

If you think, "I'll never get old in my entire life…"

"I'll always remain young in my entire life…"

"I'll never die…"

"I'll live forever in this world…"

Then, you're absolutely wrong.

This is the law of this world: you'll become old with the changing times; you'll never remain young forever in your life; you'll never live forever in this world; you'll definitely die one day. This is the ultimate truth of this world.

Therefore, don't live in the illusion that you'll always live in this world permanently.

Your life is temporary in this world.

You're just like an actor, acting on the stage of this world. You'll have to play different roles in your life.

Sometimes, you'll have to play the role of a father or a mother.

Sometimes, you'll have to play the role of a husband or a wife.

Sometimes, you'll have to play the role of a son or a daughter.

Sometimes, you'll have to play the role of a brother or a sister.

Sometimes, you'll have to play the role of an uncle or an aunt.

Sometimes, you'll have to play the role of a friend or a well-wisher.

Ask yourself the following questions:

"Am I playing a good role of a father or a mother?"

Give your answers in Yes/No

....

"Am I playing a good role as a husband or a wife?"

Give your answers in Yes/No

....

"Am I playing a good role as a son or a daughter?"

Give your answers in Yes/No

....

"Am I playing a good role as an uncle or an aunt?"

Give your answers in Yes/No

....

"Am I playing a good role as a friend or a well-wisher?"

Give your answers in Yes/No

....

How long you've played the different roles in your life is not important for you, but how beautifully and wonderfully you've played the roles in your life.

Don't count the duration of your lifespan, but count the good deeds you've delivered in your life.

Don't count the duration of your lifespan, but count the greatest impacts you've left behind in your life.

Don't count the duration of your lifespan, but count how many times you've brought changes to the lives of other people.

Don't count the duration of your lifespan, but count the blessings you've given to the people in your life.

Q. Can you live permanently in this world?

Yes, of course.

With your good deeds, you can live permanently in this world.

With your great works, you can live permanently in this world.

With your kind service to all mankind, you can live permanently in this world.

You're mortal, but only your noble deeds will make you immortal in this world.

Points to remember:

* Don't love anything too seriously.

* Don't attach too much to anything or anybody.

* Control your mind, body, and soul.

* Don't be carried away by your wildest desires and wishes.

* Don't worry too much.

* Value yourself.

* You're the most important person in your life.

* Try to live in the present moment.

* Cherish your skills and talents.

* Only your best qualities will always remain with you.

* Focus only on your work.

* Always remember that nothing will remain permanently in this world.

* Everything will come to an end when its final time arrives.

Your life is temporary in this world.

You're just like an actor, acting on the stage of this world.

You'll have to play different roles in your life.

2. Look Your Problems Beyond

"I've a family problem..."

"I've a financial problem..."

"I've a health problem..."

"I've a problem with my husband/wife..."

"I've a problem with my children..."

"I've a problem with my parents..."

"I've a problem with my boss..."

"I've a problem with my colleagues..."

"I've a problem with my relatives..."

"We've a problem with our neighbors..."

These are the basic problems of our day-to-day life. You can't deny that you're going through the problems mentioned above. You'll face one of these problems at some point in your life.

You have to keep in mind that problems are a part of your life. You'll always find yourself in the midst of problems. You can't escape from the problems of your life. But you have to solve your own problems. You have to find the right solutions to your problems. Nobody can solve the problems of your life.

You'll never find anyone in this entire world who has no problems at all. There is no one in this world. You'll only find such a person in the graveyard.

Only the dead have no problems in this world.

You're not a dead man. You're alive in this world. And as long as you're alive in this world, your problems will also be alive along with you. You can't hand over your problems to the shoulders of other people. You've got to solve your own problems. It's your own responsibility to solve your own problems.

You'll never isolate yourself from the problems of your life. You've got to face them and solve them. The more you solve your own problems, the stronger and more mature you'll become in your life. You'll know the real formula to solve the problems of your life. You'll know the real art of living your life.

If you have a family problem, then who will solve your problem?

If you have a financial problem, then who will solve your problem?

If you have a health problem, then who will solve your problem?

If you have a problem with your spouse, then who will solve your problem?

If you have a problem with your children, then who will solve your problem?

If you have a problem with your parents, then who will solve your problem?

If you have a problem with your boss, then who will solve your problem?

If you have a problem with your colleagues, then who will solve your problem?

If you have a problem with your relatives, then who will solve your problem?

If you have a problem with your neighbor, then who will solve your problem?

You're the only person who will solve your own problems. Nobody will help you solve your own problems. You have to take the initial step to solve your own problems. You have to find the right ways to solve your own problems. You can solve every problem in your life if you are really determined to solve your problems.

Points to remember:

* Look at the root causes of your problems.

* Don't be scared of your problems.

* Face your problems bravely.

* You can only solve your problems by facing them.

* Don't try to escape from your problems.

* Don't compare your problems with those of other people.

* Your problems are different from those of other people.

* Find out the right solutions to your own problems.

* Don't try to solve your problems in one go.

* Solve your problems one by one, step by step.

* First, solve your easy problems, and then solve your hardest problems.

* Don't give up if you fail to solve your problems.

* Take your time, and keep your cool and calm to solve your problems.

* Don't make your problems bigger than your life.

You'll never find anyone in this entire world who
has no problems at all.

There is no one in this world.

You'll only find such a person in the graveyard.

3. Control Yourself

Can you control yourself?

If your answer is yes, then you can do anything in your life. You not only can control yourself, but you can also control other people.

But if your answer is no, then sooner or later your life will go out of control. Once your life goes out of control, the tempest of problems and difficulties will strike in your life one after another.

Can you control your mind?

If your answer is yes, then you can manage yourself in every situation of your life.

But if your answer is no, then you can't manage anything in your life.

Your mind is faster than the speed of the wind and the speed of light. Within a nanosecond, it'll reach the Moon; within a microsecond, it'll reach any corner of the universe.

There is tremendous power in your mind. If you learn how to control your mind and utilize it in the right direction, it'll create wonder and magic for you. You can achieve everything in your life.

Never allow your mind to control you. Control your own mind. Be the master of your own mind, but don't be the slave of your own mind.

Can you control your thoughts? If your answer is yes, then you can maintain balance in your life, no matter what happens. You'll become disciplined. But if your answer is no, then your life will become imbalanced. Your thoughts are the makers of your life. You're the byproduct of your own thoughts. You'll become the way your thoughts are. Before you do anything, your thoughts arise in your mind.

If your thoughts are positive, your mindset will automatically become positive. On the other hand, if your thoughts are negative, your mindset will automatically become negative.

Can you control your emotions?

If your answer is yes, then you'll always be happy and content in your life.

But if your answer is no, then you'll always be unhappy and discontent.

Your emotions will only drive you towards grief, anxiety, and stress. If you become emotional in your life, you'll never make any hard decisions. You'll never be practical in your life.

Your life is always shaped by your hard decisions and practical approaches, not by your emotional feelings and sentiments.

Don't be swept away by the flow of your emotions. Control your emotions.

Can you control your actions?

If your answer is yes, then you'll always be successful in your life.

But if your answer is no, then you'll always be a failure in your life.

Your actions are the main characteristics of your life. Nothing will happen without your actions. One right action will enrich your entire life, and one wrong action will spoil your entire life.

Your actions decide your life. Your actions decide your success and failure. Good actions lead to good results. Bad actions lead to bad results.

Can you control your habits? If your answer is yes, then you'll always witness your growth and development. But if your answer is no, then you'll always witness your downfall and failure. Your habits will show your personality. If you cultivate good habits, you'll improve your own life. But if you cultivate bad habits, you'll ruin your own life. It is quite easy to adopt bad habits in your life, but it is very tough to get rid of them. Your bad habits are like parasites; they'll eat up your best qualities. Your bad habits always lead you to destruction. Therefore, always be aware of your bad habits.

Can you control your desires and wishes?

If your answer is yes, then you'll be able to save yourself from the fires of unnecessary things in your life.

But if your answer is no, then you'll burn yourself in the fires of unwanted things in your life.

Never allow your desires and wishes to cross their limits. Don't make them wild, since there are no limits to your desires and wishes. They are like untamed beasts, ready to wander anywhere.

Can you control your anger?

If your answer is yes, then you'll conquer all the happiness, peace, and prosperity in the entire world.

But if your answer is no, then you'll burn yourself.

Your anger is the most dangerous thing in your life; it'll not only burn your life, but it'll also burn your beautiful world. Your anger is the source of all miseries.

Put off the burning fire of your anger as soon as possible, before it consumes you and turns your beautiful life into a heap of black ashes.

Always remember that anger is just one word short of danger.

ANGER → DANGER

Can you control your hatred?

If your answer is yes, then you can spread the fragrance of love, compassion, and harmony in your own life.

But if your answer is no, then you'll drag yourself into the dark cell of unhappiness and anxiety.

Your hatred is like a disease. Once it spreads in your life, it will not only kill you, but it will also kill all the beautiful relationships in your life.

Your hatred is the main cause of disunity and disputes in your life. Never allow the weeds of hatred to sprout in your life. The moment it sprouts, uproot it as soon as possible. Your hatred is the enemy of your love, compassion, unity, happiness, and peace.

Can you control your jealousy?

If your answer is yes, then you'll always find enough time to enjoy and develop yourself in your life.

But if your answer is no, then you'll always find yourself tense and stressed. Your jealousy will only steal your happiness and peace. The moment the virus of jealousy makes a host in your life, it will kill you first, before it kills other people. Your jealousy is like a poison. It will poison your mind, body, and soul. It will poison your dreams, thoughts, ideas, plans, decisions, and actions. It will poison your beautiful life.

Give up your jealousy. You have no right to view the lives of other people with the eyes of jealousy. If you're jealous, you're just wasting your valuable time. You can't achieve anything in your life.

Can you control your greed? If your answer is yes, then you can earn wealth and prosper in your life.

But if your answer is no, then you can't earn anything in your life. You'll only become penniless. You'll become bankrupt.

If you become greedy, you'll always witness your loss. You'll only lose your hard-earned money when you become greedy. Don't gamble anything in your life, but whatever you do, do it like a wise businessman.

It is not the game of gambling that wipes out all the wealth of a person, but it is only his greed that wipes out everything.

Can you control your lust?

If your answer is yes, then you'll achieve everything in your life.

But if your answer is no, then you'll never achieve anything in your life.

Your lust will make you blind. It'll force you to act on anything without thinking. It'll kill your conscience. It'll make you intoxicated. You'll lose your own mind. You'll become its slave. You'll start following its commands blindly.

Your lust is the main reason for your downfall and failure. Your lust always leads you to the door of hell. Once you trap yourself in the web of lust, you'll never rescue yourself in your entire life. You'll fall deep into the ditch of sins and crimes.

Points to remember:

* Only you can control yourself.

* Nobody can control you.

* Never allow anyone to control you.

* Don't try to become a puppet in the hands of other people.

* Only you can control your thoughts.

* Only you can control your mind.

* Only you can control your desires and wishes.

* Only you can control your emotions.

* Only you can control your actions.

* Only you can control your habits.

* Only you can control your anger.

* Only you can control your hatred.

* Only you can control your jealousy.

* Only you can control your greed.

* Only you can control your lust.

* You're the only person who can control yourself.

* Be the master of your own life.

Nobody can control you.

Only you can control yourself.

Never allow anyone to control you.

Don't try to become a puppet in the hands of other people.

4. Keep Your Mind, Body and Spirit in Unison

Your mind says, "I am weak and tired."

Your body reacts, "Yes, I am also weak and tired like you."

Your spirit responds, "Yes, I, too, feel the same as you both."

The way your mind will act, in the same way your body will react, and the way your body will react, in the same way your spirit will respond.

MIND (weak/tired) ⇆ BODY (weak/tired) ⇆ SPIRIT (weak/tired)

If your mind is tired, your body will automatically get tired, and it'll be unable to work for you.

If your body is tired, your spirit will automatically get tired, and it'll be unable to work for you.

If your body and spirit are tired, your mind will automatically get tired, and it'll be unable to work for you.

Whenever you speak something good or bad/positive or negative to yourself, your mind will become active to accept your good or bad/positive or negative words, and at the same time, your body will release dopamine according to your words in your brain. Then, your mind and spirit will respond to you.

(Dopamine is a chemical found naturally in the human body. It is a neurotransmitter, meaning it sends signals from the body to the brain.)

Body

(Dopamine)

⇩

Brain

⇩

Mind

⇩

Spirit

Your mind, body, and spirit will always work in unison.

You can't separate your mind, body, and spirit.

They are always working together.

They always complement each other.

When your mind, body, and spirit work together, you can focus on anything.

→You'll be able to do anything in your life.

→Everything will become possible for you.

→You can do miracles in your life.

→You can achieve everything in your life.

→You can transform yourself the way you want in your life.

→Your mind will work like a magic wand for you.

→Your body will always be ready to do anything for you.

→Your spirit will always be ready to help you.

→You can discover anything in your life.

→You can invent anything in your life.

→You can create anything in your life.

→You can develop anything in your life.

→You can build anything in your life.

Points to remember:

* Always think positively.

* Always think good things about yourself.

* Always love yourself.

* Try to live a disciplined life.

* Control yourself (emotions and actions).

* Cultivate good habits.

* Learn to enjoy yourself.

* Be happy and content with yourself.

* Always analyze yourself as well as your daily work.

* Avoid bad company.

* Avoid bad habits like smoking and drinking.

* Practice regular meditation and yoga.

* Always be optimistic in your life.

When your mind, body, and spirit work together,
you can focus on anything. You'll be able to do anything
in your life. Nothing is impossible for you.

5. Control Your Ego

"I'm only the king of this world."

"I am only the strongest and mightiest man in this world."

"I can only rule this entire world."

"I'm only the winner."

"Nobody can defeat me."

"Nobody is like me."

"I am only the richest man in this world."

"I'm only the master of everything."

"Nothing will happen to me."

"I'm only the most learned man in this world."

"I'm only the most talented man in this world."

"I'm only the clearest man in this world."

"I'm only the most handsome man in this world."

"I'm only the most beautiful woman in this universe."

If any one of the above statements ever arises in your mind, then you're suffering from the most deadly virus called "Self-ego." Once your ego attacks your mind, it'll automatically attack your good thoughts, good ideas, good plans, good decisions, and good actions. You'll be completely infected by the virus of your ego.

You'll start behaving as if nobody is like you. You'll only think about yourself. You'll only know your own benefits. You'll become selfish. You'll never listen to anyone. You'll become arrogant.

The moment you become egoistic, your downfall will begin. Then be ready to witness your downfall and failure. Your life will become like hell.

And once you fall due to your ego, nobody will rescue you. You'll have to face its hard consequences. Your destruction is one hundred percent certain.

In the great epic of Ramayana, the demon king Ravana was born as a Brahmin. He was a greatly learned Brahmin. He had complete knowledge of the Vedas. He was a great devotee of Lord Shiva. He had a boon from Lord Brahma that no living being, whether gods or goddesses, whether devils or demons, would ever kill him.

Ravana had a false pride and ego, believing that nobody in the entire universe could ever defeat him. He started tormenting the entire earth, netherworld, and heaven altogether.

However, he had forgotten that only a mere human being would defeat him. Then, Lord Vishnu himself reincarnated in human form and took birth as Lord Rama.

Ravana became so arrogant and egoistic that he kidnapped Lord Rama's wife, Sita, who was also the reincarnation of Goddess Lakshmi.

Ravana's brother Vibhishana pleaded with him to return Lord Rama's wife, Sita, with due respect and honor. But Ravana didn't listen to Vibhishana and banished him from Lanka. As a result, Ravana was killed by Lord Rama's hands in the furious battle. Ravana's false pride and ego didn't only kill him but also killed his dear sons and brothers; he himself destroyed his mighty kingdom.

If you want to achieve happiness, contentment, peace, success, and prosperity in your life, then give up your ego.

→ Give up your ego; you'll get nothing in your life.

→ Give up your ego; you'll only get unhappiness, discontentment, anxiety, failure, and destruction in your life.

→ Give up your ego before it poisons your mind, body, and spirit.

→ Give up your ego before it erodes your knowledge and wisdom.

→ Give up your ego before it completely ruins your life.

→ Give up your ego before it completely steals your happiness and peace.

Points to remember:

* Always be humble in your life.

* Accept your mistakes gladly.

* Respect your fellow mates as you respect your loved ones.

* Try to understand the feelings of other people.

* Take good advice from your well-wishers.

* Try to listen to the viewpoints of other people.

* Don't speculate or assume anything without knowing its reality.

* Don't underestimate anybody in your life.

* Don't react to anything too quickly.

* Don't make any decisions in haste.

Your ego is the biggest enemy of your growth and development in your life. Your ego is the root cause of your failure, downfall, and destruction. Give up your ego as soon as possible. Otherwise, it'll swallow your beautiful life.

6. Suppress Your Anger

Have you ever thought about the origin of your anger?

Your answer may be yes or no.

When you desire something, but for some reason, you're unable to fulfill it.

When you wish for something, but for some reason, you're unable to fulfill it.

When you expect something, but for some reason, you're unable to fulfill it.

When you dream of something, but for some reason, you're unable to fulfill it.

When you want something, but for some reason, you're unable to fulfill it.

When you need something, but for some reason, you're unable to fulfill it.

When you want to do something, but somebody has stopped you.

When you want to go somewhere, but somebody has stopped you.

In the above-mentioned situations, how can you deal with yourself?

Either you'll accept the situations, or you'll react.

If you accept the situations, you can handle yourself very easily, no matter what happens. You'll remain cool and calm.

On the contrary, if you react against the situations, you can't handle yourself. You'll get angry. And when you get angry, you'll ruin your own life. You'll invite your own unhappiness, anxieties, and destruction into your life.

Hundreds and thousands of different situations will occur in your everyday life, one after another. Some situations are very serious and tough. Some situations are very challenging and nail-biting. They will create an impossible task for you.

Can you stop them all?

No.

You can't stop them all.

You'll have to accept them.

You'll only handle them when you remain cool and calm.

You'll never handle any situation when you get angry.

But you'll only multiply your own problems when you get angry.

Your anger is the biggest enemy of your life.

→ Your anger will burn down your beautiful life.

→ Your anger will spoil your wonderful life.

→ Your anger will burn your mind, body, and soul.

→ Your anger will make you blind.

→ Your anger will burn down your thoughts, knowledge, and wisdom.

→ Your anger will kill your conscience.

If you get angry, you'll commit a great blunder in your life.

You'll dig your own graveyard.

You'll invite your own downfall and destruction.

You'll be unable to think good things.

You'll be unable to make good plans.

You'll be unable to make good decisions.

You'll be unable to prepare yourself.

You'll be unable to act in the right direction.

You'll be unable to achieve anything in your life.

You can handle your anger in the following ways:

→ Accept the situations of your life.

→ Don't react with anything/anybody.

→ Minimize your desires.

→ Control your wishes.

→ Control your emotions.

→ Stop expecting too much from others.

→ Always rely on yourself.

→ Never depend on anybody.

→ You should know the difference between your needs and wants.

→ You should know which things are important to you and which things are unimportant to you.

→ Maintain your own decorum.

Practical approaches to handle your anger:

1. Whenever you get angry, close your eyes and start counting backward from 100 to 1.

(E.g., 100…99…98…1)

2. Whenever you get angry, look at your toes for a minute.

3. Whenever you get angry, drink a glassful of water slowly, as if you're swallowing your anger.

4. Whenever you get angry, take a cold bath or a cool shower.

5. Whenever you get angry, chant some mantras like:

* "Om Shanti!… Om Shanti!… Om Shanti!"

* "Hari Om!… Hari Om!… Hari Om!"

* "Om Namah Shivaya!… Om Namah Shivaya!… Om Namah Shivaya!"

6. Whenever you get angry, ask yourself:

"Why am I getting angry?"

"What is the reason for my anger?"

* Repeat the same question five to ten times until you get the right answers.

7. Whenever you get angry, self-affirm yourself:

"Cool down... Calm down..."

"I am a cool and calm person..."

"I am happy with myself..."

"I am satisfied with myself..."

"I am a peaceful soul..."

8. Whenever you get angry, laugh aloud.

9. Whenever you get angry, listen to your favorite songs or watch your favorite comedy movies.

10. Whenever you get angry, go for a long walk.

* Note: Whenever you get angry, never ride your bike; never drive your car.

Points to remember:

* Learn to pacify yourself.

* Control your wildest desires and wishes.

* Learn to listen to your conscience.

* Try to do what is right for you.

* Don't be carried away by the winds of your emotions.

* Engage in regular contemplation.

* Before you make any decision, think deeply and judge it.

* Don't be serious in your approach, but maintain your cool and calm.

* Be happy and content with yourself.

* Always try to behave in a mature way.

Your anger is the biggest enemy of your life.

It will burn down your beautiful life.

It will spoil your wonderful life.

It will burn your mind, body, and soul.

7. Remove Your Unwanted Desires

Your unwanted desires are like the two uncontrollable horses of a chariot. They will drive you wherever they want if you're unable to control them. But if you're able to control your unwanted desires, they will never drive you anywhere without your consent.

You're the charioteer of your own life. Only you can control the uncontrollable desires of your life.

If you have any unwanted desires, you'll definitely witness your downfall sooner or later in your life. Your unwanted desires will lead you in such a way that you'll not only forget your real identity but also lead you to commit sinful and illegal acts.

Once, a man was very happy and content in his small house. He was always happy and peaceful. He was an honest man. But one day, he desired to build a big house, even though his earnings were meager. He knew that it was just his unwanted desire.

In order to fulfill this unwanted desire, he wanted to earn more money and wealth. Then he managed to earn more money and wealth by doing some unfair means, and he built a big house for himself.

But after some time, he desired to build a big mansion. He needed more money and wealth to fulfill this unwanted desire. Then, again, he started earning more money and wealth by using illegal means. And he built a big mansion for himself.

When he started living in his newly built mansion, he didn't find happiness and peace. His mind was disturbed and full of tension and stress because of his wrongdoings. His conscience didn't allow him to live in happiness and peace. Then, he realized that he was happy and peaceful when he used to live in his small house. He also realized that his unwanted desires had forced him to use unfair means and engage in illegal activities. His heavenly life turned into hell. Every now and then, he lived his life in fear and guilt. He had to spend his life like a convict.

Q What are your unwanted desires?

→Your unwanted desires are the desires that are of no use to you.

→Your unwanted desires are wild and childish.

→Your unwanted desires force you to do anything.

→Your unwanted desires do not know what is right for you and what is wrong for you.

→Your unwanted desires make you blind.

→Your unwanted desires make you selfish.

→Your unwanted desires are the desires that exceed their limits.

→Your unwanted desires are the desires that make you spend your hard-earned money on unnecessary things.

→Your unwanted desires are the desires that make you live in a superficial world.

→Your unwanted desires are the desires that only give you instant gratification.

→Your unwanted desires are the desires that lead you to commit acts without your consent.

→Your unwanted desires are the desires that lead you to unhappiness and anxiety.

Q. How can you control your unwanted desires?

→ Check your unwanted desires, whether they are for good things or bad things.

→ Check your unwanted desires to see which direction they will lead you.

→ Check your unwanted desires before they bring you any trouble.

→ Check your unwanted desires before they manipulate your mind.

→ Check your unwanted desires before they force you to do anything wrong.

→ Check your unwanted desires before they make you their slave.

Your unwanted desires are like unwanted weeds in fertile land. If you do not remove your unwanted desires, they will spoil your beautiful life.

Points to remember:

* Always try to make the right decisions.

* Not everything is important to you.

* Only focus on the important things.

* Only focus on the good things in your life.

* Try to differentiate between your good habits and bad habits.

* Always try to cultivate good hobbies.

* Always try to choose the right path for yourself.

* Always avoid the wrong people and wrong things.

* Don't compare yourself to other people.

* Be specific about your wants and needs.

* Always be responsible in your life.

If you're unable to control your unwanted desires,
they will lead you to your downfall and destruction.

8. Get Rid of Bad Thoughts

"I hate him/her."

"I don't like him/her."

"I'll harm him/her."

"I'll ruin his life… I'll ruin her life."

"He is bad… She is bad…"

"He is my enemy… She is my enemy."

"I'll kill him/her."

"I'll take revenge against him/her."

"I'll never forgive him/her."

"I'm bad."

"I'm not a wise boy/girl/man/woman."

"I'm not good at anything."

"I'm a useless person."

"I'm weak."

"I'm alone in this world."

"I'll quit!"

"I'll kill myself."

All the above statements are bad thoughts.

These bad thoughts will only bring you self-destruction.

These bad thoughts are like a poison.

These bad thoughts will only misguide you.

These bad thoughts will only lead you to downfall and failure.

These bad thoughts will make you worried and stressed.

These bad thoughts will wear out your self-belief and self-confidence.

Whenever such bad thoughts arise in your mind, replace them with good and positive thoughts, such as:

"I love him/her."

"I do like him/her."

"I'll care for him/her."

"I'll improve his life… I'll improve her life."

"He is good… She is good…"

"He is my friend… She is my friend."

"I'll help him/her."

“I’ll support him/her.”

“I’ll forgive him/her.”

“I’m good.”

“I’m a wise boy/girl/man/woman.”

“I’m good at everything.”

“I’m strong.”

“I’m a valuable person.”

“I’m not alone in this world.”

“I’ll never give up!”

“I love myself.”

Your bad thoughts are like poison. They will kill your good thoughts. They will bring negative thoughts to your mind. They will create a negative mindset. They will foster a negative attitude.

Always be aware of your bad thoughts. One bad thought can destroy your entire life, while one good thought can boost your entire life.

How do your bad thoughts arise in your mind?

→ Your bad thoughts arise in your mind when you feel lonely in your life.

→ Your bad thoughts arise in your mind when your wishes and desires are not fulfilled.

→ Your bad thoughts arise in your mind when somebody hurts you.

→ Your bad thoughts arise in your mind when somebody plays with your emotions.

→ Your bad thoughts arise in your mind when somebody betrays you.

→ Your bad thoughts arise in your mind when you face defeat and failure in your life.

How can you get rid of your bad thoughts?

→ Whenever any bad thoughts arise in your mind, think only positive things.

→ Whenever you feel alone, go to your closest friend and share your feelings.

→ Write down all the bad thoughts that arise in your mind.

→ Let your bad thoughts flow away from your mind in the form of words and sentences.

Ask yourself the following questions:

1Q → "Why am I thinking these bad thoughts?"

2Q → "What is the use of these bad thoughts in my life?"

3Q → "What are the reasons for these bad thoughts?"

4Q → "Where do these bad thoughts lead me in my life?"

5Q → "Am I doing the right thing by allowing these bad thoughts in my life?"

Ask yourself the same questions again and again.

You'll get your right answers.

If your desires and wishes are not fulfilled,

Don't worry.

Accept it gladly.

Your desires and wishes will be fulfilled one day.

Be optimistic.

But never bring bad thoughts to your mind.

If somebody hurts you,

Don't worry.

Forgive him/her.

Time will heal everything.

Everything will be all right one day.

But never bring bad thoughts to your mind.

If somebody plays with your emotions,

Don't worry.

Let him/her do so.

Control your emotions and love yourself.

They will understand your feelings one day.

But never bring bad thoughts to your mind.

If somebody betrays you,

Don't worry.

Let him/her do so.

Don't feel bad.

Your good time will definitely arrive one day.

But never bring bad thoughts to your mind.

If you face defeat and failure,

Don't worry.

Try again and again.

Never give up.

You'll succeed in your endeavors one day.

But never bring bad thoughts to your mind.

Points to remember:

* Always control your thoughts.

* Never allow your thoughts to wander.

* Give proper direction to your thoughts.

* Train your thoughts like the best trainer.

* Guide your thoughts onto the right path.

* Watch your thoughts every day.

* Judge your thoughts every day.

* Analyze your thoughts every day.

* Read your thoughts every day.

* Lead your thoughts every day.

* Nourish your thoughts with great ideas and plans.

* Grow and nurture your thoughts with great knowledge and wisdom.

Your bad thoughts are like poison.

They will kill your best thoughts.

They will kill your best ideas.

They will kill your best plans.

9. Maintain Cool and Calm

Close your eyes and try to watch your thoughts silently.

Just try to watch your thoughts.

Don't do anything.

Do you feel cool and calm in your mind?

Is your mind cool and calm?

What kinds of thoughts do you feel inside your mind?

You'll find thousands of random thoughts in your mind. But none of these thoughts are linked with each other. These random thoughts are like the continuous rising and falling waves in the ocean.

There is no end to these random thoughts. Out of 100% of thoughts, only 0.99% of your thoughts are useful for you, and the rest are like junk items. No use.

These random and junk thoughts are like naughty monkeys, always ready to fight with each other or to attack each other. None of these thoughts will complement each other.

These random and junk thoughts will never allow your mind to remain cool and calm. They will never allow your mind to think constructive ideas. These random and junk thoughts will create blockages for your new ideas and thoughts.

For instance, do you see the crowded marketplace, how the shopkeepers and the customers are dealing with each other? In the midst of the crowded marketplace, you'll neither speak nor hear anything. Your mind will get disturbed by the unwanted buzz.

In a similar way, your random and junk thoughts will create the exact scene of a crowded marketplace inside your mind. In such a scenario, you can't maintain cool and calm in your mind. Your mind will get annoyed with these random and junk thoughts.

These random and junk thoughts will make your mind like a dustbin.

Do you want to make your mind like a dustbin?

No.

Nobody wants to make his or her mind like a dustbin.

Therefore, don't make your mind the dustbin of random and junk thoughts.

These random and junk thoughts will only steal your cool and calmness. Clean it up as soon as possible, before it spoils your mind, body, and soul.

How can you keep your mind cool and calm?

→ You have to remove all these random and junk thoughts from your mind.

→ You have to throw away all these unwanted and unnecessary thoughts from your mind.

→ You have to delete all these random and junk thoughts from your mind.

→ You have to reprogram your mind.

→ You have to keep yourself busy with some purposeful work.

→ You have to fill your mind with new ideas/thoughts.

→ You have to fill your mind with creative ideas/thoughts.

→ You have to fill your mind with productive ideas/thoughts.

→ You have to fill your mind with progressive ideas/thoughts.

→ Do meditation regularly.

→ Stop overthinking.

→ Don't react to anything/anybody.

→ Don't allow any negative thoughts to enter your mind.

→ Learn to balance your life.

→ Always feed your mind with great thoughts, great ideas, great lessons, great knowledge, and great wisdom.

Points to remember:

* Learn to silence your random and junk thoughts.

* Learn to maintain yourself.

* Learn to concentrate on yourself.

* Learn to safeguard your mind from unwanted distractions.

* Learn to reprogram your mind.

* Learn to think new, creative, productive, and progressive thoughts.

You'll only keep your mind cool and calm when you're able to silence the random and junk thoughts.

10. Do Your Research

"What do I want to do in my life?"

"What are the aims and objectives of my life?"

"In which field do I want to join in my near future?"

"Which is the right career suitable for me?"

"Am I ready to do this?"

These are the questions you'll have to ask yourself before you decide to do anything in your life.

The next step is to find out what exactly you want to do in your life.

Then, you have to research yourself in your chosen field.

And once your research is complete in your chosen field, go for it.

Give your mind, body, and soul.

Give your complete focus to your job.

Persevere.

Nobody will dare to stop you.

There is a 100% guarantee of your success.

When you research yourself in your chosen field, the following things will help you:

→ You'll know your own caliber.

→ You'll know how to grow and develop yourself.

→ You'll know whether your choice is right or wrong.

→ You'll know whether you're the right candidate or not.

→ You'll know what challenges you'll have to face.

→ You'll know what sacrifices you'll have to make.

→ You'll know what kind of potential you require.

→ You'll know your strong points and weak points.

→ You'll know how to conquer your doubts and fears.

→ You'll know how to prepare yourself.

→ You'll know how to adjust yourself to tough situations.

→ You'll know how to make your plans.

→ You'll know how to utilize your valuable time.

→ You'll know how to use your ideas and thoughts.

→ You'll know how long you'll have to struggle to reach your final goal.

→ You'll easily identify your own opportunities.

However, if you chase your chosen field without doing any research, you'll face the following hurdles:

→ You'll lose yourself in the midst of the crowd.

→ You'll always find yourself standing in long queues along with thousands of competitors.

→ You'll act like a blind person.

→ You'll always wander aimlessly in your life.

→ You'll be manipulated by other people very easily.

→ You'll become like a copycat.

→ You'll be unable to adjust yourself to the changing environment.

→ You'll always be confused and fearful.

→ You'll face problems at every step.

→ You'll be unable to prepare yourself.

→ You'll be unable to plan anything.

→ You'll waste your valuable time and money.

› You'll find everything turning against you.

→ You'll trap yourself in a vicious cycle.

→ You'll have no idea when you'll reach your final destination.

→ You'll be unable to identify your opportunities.

→ You'll witness your failure.

Therefore, whatever you do in your life, first of all, do your own research; then proceed further to execute.

It's only your research that will help you in every field.

Don't try to do anything without doing your own research.

Points to remember:

* Don't forget to do your own research.

* Don't hesitate to ask anything.

* Your research is the first criterion to do anything.

* Your research will always guide you.

* Your research will always help you know your own potential.

* Don't take a single step on anything without doing your own research.

* Don't follow the paths of other people.

* Make the roadmap for your own success.

* Don't depend on anybody.

* Be your own teacher; be your own guide; and be your own leader.

* Nobody will research anything better than you.

* You're the best researcher of your own life.

It's only your research that will help you in every field. Don't try to do anything without doing your own research

About the author:

Birister Sharma is a full time author. He is also an avid reader. He loves reading, writing, and motivation. He has penned down dozens of self-help motivational books and novels so far.

You may contact him @ birister2007@gmail.com

www.ingramcontent.com/pod-product-compliance
Lightning Source LLC
Chambersburg PA
CBHW040743120726
48007CB00007B/76